MAGIC TIME

STUDENT BOOK 1

Kathleen Kampa

Charles Vilina

OXFORD

UNIVERSITY PRESS

OXFORD
UNIVERSITY PRESS

198 Madison Avenue
New York, NY 10016 USA

Great Clarendon Street
Oxford OX2 6DP England

Oxford New York

Auckland Cape Town Dar es Salaam Hong Kong Karachi
Kuala Lumpur Madrid Melbourne Mexico City Nairobi
New Delhi Shanghai Taipei Toronto
With offices in
Argentina Austria Brazil Chile Czech Republic France Greece
Guatemala Hungary Italy Japan South Korea Poland Portugal
Singapore Switzerland Thailand Turkey Ukraine Vietnam

OXFORD is a trademark of Oxford University Press.

ISBN-13: 978-0-19-436180-4
ISBN-10: 0-19-436180-2

Library of Congress Cataloging-in-Publication Data

Kampa, Kathleen.
   Magic time student book 1 / Kathleen Kampa, Charles Vilina.
      p. cm.
   Includes index.
      ISBN 0-19-436180-2 (v. 1)
      1. English language—Textbooks for foreign speakers— Juvenile
literature. [1. English language—Textbooks for foreign speakers.]
I. Vilina, Charles. II. Title

PE1128.K283 2001
428.2'4—dc21   2001036130

Editorial Manager: Shelagh Speers
Senior Editor: Lesley Koustaff
Editor: Paul Phillips
Senior Production Editor: Joseph McGasko
Elementary Design Manager: Doris Chen Pinzon
Designer: Ruby Harn
Art Buyers: Patricia Marx, Jodi Waxman
Production Manager: Shanta Persaud
Production Coordinator: Eve Wong

Musical arrangements and chant music: William Hirtz

Illustrations: Lynn Adams, Cathy Beylon, Bill Colrus,
Anthony Lewis/JK Portfolio, Inc., Tammie Lyon, Dana Regan,
Jamie Smith/HK Portfolio, Inc., Jim Talbot

Original characters developed by Amy Wummer

Cover design: Silver Editions
Cover illustrations: Cheryl Mendenhall and Jim Talbot

Printing (last digit): 10 9 8 7 6

Printed in China

*Our sincere gratitude to our editors Lesley Koustaff and Paul Phillips
for patiently directing our energies and believing in our vision for
Magic Time. Special thanks to our sons John and Christian, as well as
to our parents, for their enduring love and support. Finally, to our
many students, to whom Magic Time is dedicated, thank you for
making teaching the greatest profession in the world.*

– Kathleen Kampa and Charles Vilina

Table of Contents

Syllabus

Unit	*Title*/Topic	Word Time	Use The Words	Action Word Time	Use The Action Words
I	*New Friends/* Names	Annie Ted Digger Dot	Hello! I'm Ted.	smile wave shake hands nod	Let's shake hands.
2	*At the Beach/* Shapes	triangle circle star rectangle heart square	I see a star.	walk dive tiptoe swim	Dive over here.
3	*Colorful Jungle/* Colors	blue red yellow green black orange	It's black.	draw color write paint	Paint with me.
Review I					
Spring ABCs		**a**pple, **b**ear, **c**at, **d**og, **e**lephant, **f**ish			
4	*In the Classroom/* Classroom Items	pencil book ruler eraser book bag crayon	It's a ruler.	pick up your book put down your book open your book bag close your book bag	Put down your book slowly. Put down your book quickly.
5	*Dot's Birthday Party/* Numbers	I one 2 two 3 three 4 four 5 five 6 six 7 seven 8 eight 9 nine I0 ten	I'm one year old. I'm six years old.	stand up sit down kneel down lie down	Lie down. Okay.
6	*Painting a Mural/* Parts of the Body	arms legs hands feet fingers toes	I have two hands.	wash your hands dry your hands brush your hair comb your hair	Please brush your hair.
Review 2					
Summer ABCs		**g**oat, **h**orse, **i**guana, **j**uice, **k**angaroo, **l**emon, **m**onkey			

Unit	*Title*/Topic	**Word Time**	**Use The Words**	**Action Word Time**	**Use The Action Words**
7	*At the Campsite/* Feelings	hot cold thirsty hungry sleepy tired	I'm cold.	drink eat cook clean up	Let's eat together.
8	*Fruits and Vegetables Show/* Fruits and Vegetables	tomatoes bananas carrots oranges cucumbers apples	I like oranges.	clap shout sing dance	Sing with me. Sure.
9	*At the Park/*Actions	swim play soccer ride a bike jump rope play baseball climb a tree	I can climb a tree.	throw the ball catch the ball hit the ball kick the ball	Watch me catch the ball.
	Review 3				
	Fall ABCs	**n**est, **o**ctopus, **p**ig, **q**uilt, **r**abbit, **s**andwich			
10	*Pet Parade/* Pets	rabbit dog turtle bird frog cat	I love my rabbit.	fly jump hop run	It can fly.
11	*Family Fun/* Family Members	grandmother mother sister grandfather father brother	This is my grandmother.	wink whistle laugh cry	Please don't laugh. Sorry.
12	*Slumber Parties/* My Room	clock lamp pillow chair bed desk	This is a bed. That is a chair.	play read listen watch TV	Let's listen. Good idea!
	Review 4				
	Winter ABCs	**t**urtle, **u**mbrella, **v**iolin, **w**atch, **b**ox, **y**o-yo, **z**ebra			

Numbers

Word Time

A. Listen and repeat.

1.
Annie

2.
Ted

3.
Digger

4.
Dot

B. Listen and point below. Then chant.

C. Listen and write the number.

Use the Words

A. 🎵 Listen and repeat.

Hello! I'm Ted.

B. 🎵 Listen and point below.

C. 🎵 Listen and point. Then sing along.

Action Word Time

A. 🎧 Listen and repeat.

1.
smile

2.
wave

3.
shake hands

4.
nod

B. 🎧 Listen and point below. Then chant.

C. 🎧 Listen and write the number.

Use the Action Words

A. Listen and repeat.

Let's shake hands.

B. Listen and point below.

C. Listen and point. Then sing along.

Word Time

A. 🎧 Listen and repeat.

1. triangle
2. circle
3. star
4. rectangle
5. heart
6. square

B. 🎧 Listen and point below. Then chant.

C. 🎧 Listen and write the number.

Use the Words

A. 🎧 Listen and repeat.

I see a star.

B. 🎧 Listen and point below.

C. 🎧 Listen and point. Then sing along.

Action Word Time

A. 🎧 Listen and repeat.

1.
walk

2.
dive

3.
tiptoe

4.
swim

B. 🎧 Listen and point below. Then chant.

C. 🎧 Listen and write the number.

Use the Action Words

A. 💿 Listen and repeat.

B. 💿 Listen and point below.

C. 💿 Listen and point. Then sing along.

Word Time

A. Listen and repeat.

1. blue

2. red

3. yellow

4. green

5. black

6. orange

B. Listen and point below. Then chant.

C. 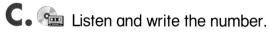 Listen and write the number.

Use the Words

A. Listen and repeat.

> It's black.

B. Listen and point below.

C. Listen and point. Then sing along.

Action Word Time

A. 🎧 Listen and repeat.

1.

draw

2.

color

3.

write

4.

paint

B. 🎧 Listen and point below. Then chant.

C. 🎧 Listen and write the number.

Use the Action Words

A. 🎧 Listen and repeat.

Paint with me.

B. 🎧 Listen and point below.

C. 🎧 Listen and point. Then sing along.

A. Listen and check.

1.

Dot   Digger

2.

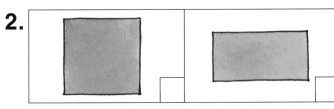

square   rectangle

3.

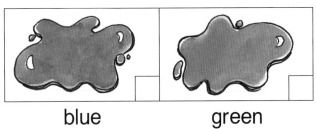

blue   green

4.

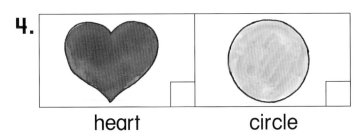

heart   circle

B. Listen and match.

1.

black

triangle

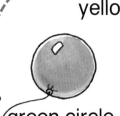
yellow star

2.

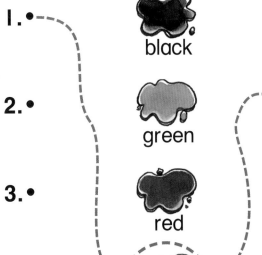
green

star

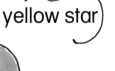
green circle

red heart

3.

red

circle

4.

yellow

square

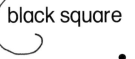
black square

blue triangle

5.

orange

heart

6.

blue

rectangle

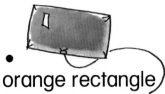
orange rectangle

A.  Listen and match.

1.
Hello! I'm Annie.

2.
It's blue.

3.
I see a rectangle.

4.
Paint with me.

5.
Let's wave!

6.
Dive over here!

Shake hands with me.

Let's swim!

Hello! I'm Dot.

Draw over here.

I see Dot.

It's a star.

B. Role play these scenes with a partner.

Spring ABCs

A. 🎧📼 Listen and repeat.

Aa — **apple**   Bb — **bear**   Cc — **ca**...

B. 🎧 Listen and point. Then chant. **C.** 🎧 Listen. Find and point below.

Dd **dog** **E**e **elephant** **F**f **fish**

Word Time

4

A. Listen and repeat.

1. pencil
2. book
3. ruler
4. eraser
5. book bag
6. crayon

B. Listen and point below. Then chant.

C. Listen and write the number.

Use the Words

A. 🔊 Listen and repeat.

B. 🔊 Listen and point below.

C. 🔊 Listen and point. Then sing along.

Action Word Time

A. Listen and repeat.

1.

pick up
your book

2.

put down
your book

3.

open your
book bag

4.

close your
book bag

B. Listen and point below. Then chant.

C. Listen and write the number.

Use the Action Words

A. 🎧 Listen and repeat.

Put down your book slowly.

Put down your book quickly.

B. 🎧 Listen and point below.

C. 🎧 Listen and point. Then sing along.

Word Time

A. 🎧 Listen and repeat.

1	2	3	4	5
one	two	three	four	five
6	7	8	9	10
six	seven	eight	nine	ten

B. 🎧 Listen and point below. Then chant.

C. 🎧 Listen and write the number.

Use the Words

A. 🎧 Listen and repeat.

I'm one year old.

I'm six years old.

B. 🎧 Listen and point below.

C. 🎧 Listen and point. Then sing along.

Action Word Time

A. 🎧 Listen and repeat.

1.

stand up

2.

sit down

3.

kneel down

4.

lie down

B. 🎧 Listen and point below. Then chant.

C. 🎧 Listen and write the number.

Use the Action Words

A. 🎧 Listen and repeat.

Lie down.

Okay.

B. 🎧 Listen and point below.

C. 🎧 Listen and point. Then sing along.

Word Time

A. Listen and repeat.

1. arms

2. legs

3. hands

4. feet

5. fingers

6. toes

B. Listen and point below. Then chant.

C. Listen and write the number.

Use the Words

A. 🎧 Listen and repeat.

I have two hands.

B. 🎧 Listen and point below.   **C.** 🎧 Listen and point. Then sing along.

Action Word Time

A. 🎧 Listen and repeat.

1.

wash your hands

2.

dry your hands

3.

brush your hair

4.

comb your hair

B. 💿 Listen and point below. Then chant.

C. 💿 Listen and write the number.

Use the Action Words

A. 📼 Listen and repeat.

Please brush your hair.

B. 📼 Listen and point below.

C. 📼 Listen and point. Then sing along.

A. Listen and check.

1.

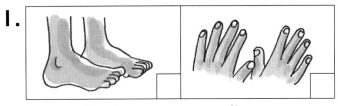

feet   fingers

2.

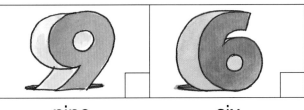

nine   six

3.

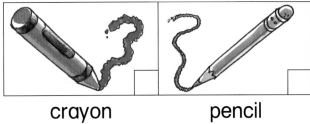

crayon   pencil

4.

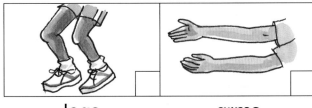

legs   arms

B. Listen and match.

1.•

2.•

3.•

4.•

5.•

rulers

hands

toes

books

book bags

four hands

seven rulers

two book bags

five books

ten toes

A. 🎧 Listen and match.

1.

It's a book.

I'm eight years old.

2.

I'm seven years old.

Stand up quickly.

3.

I have ten fingers.

Dry your feet.

4.

Open your book slowly.

Please kneel down.

5.

Wash your hands.

It's a green ruler.

6.

Please sit down.

I have six crayons.

B. Role play these scenes with a partner.

Summer ABCs

A.  Listen and repeat.

Gg **g**oat Hh **h**orse Ii **i**guana Jj

B.  Listen and point. Then chant.

C. Listen. Find and point below.

juice   **K**k   **k**angaroo   Ll   **l**emon   **M**m   **m**onkey

Word Time

7

A. Listen and repeat.

1.  hot

2. cold

3. thirsty

4. hungry

5. sleepy

6. tired

B. Listen and point below. Then chant.

C. Listen and write the number.

Use the Words

A. 🔊 Listen and repeat.

I'm cold.

B. 🔊 Listen and point below.

C. 🔊 Listen and point. Then sing along.

Action Word Time

A. 🔊 Listen and repeat.

1.

drink

2.

eat

3.

cook

4.

clean up

B. 🔊 Listen and point below. Then chant.

C. 🔊 Listen and write the number.

Use the Action Words

A. 🔊 Listen and repeat.

Let's eat together.

B. 🔊 Listen and point below.

C. 🔊 Listen and point. Then sing along.

Word Time

8

A. Listen and repeat.

1.  tomatoes
2.  bananas
3. 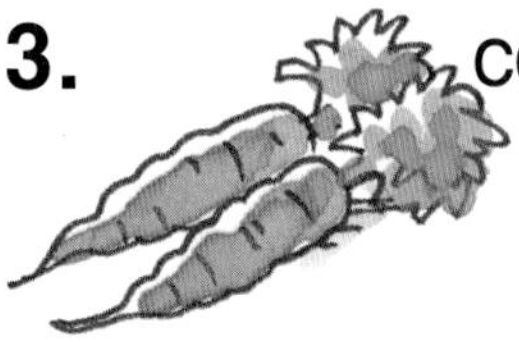 carrots
4.  oranges
5. 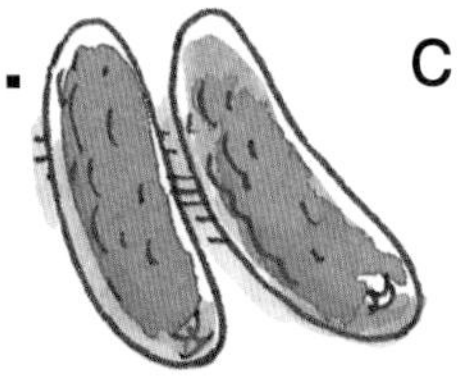 cucumbers
6.  apples

B. Listen and point below. Then chant.

C. Listen and write the number.

Use the Words

A. 📼 Listen and repeat.

I like oranges.

B. 📼 Listen and point below.

C. 📼 Listen and point. Then sing along.

Action Word Time

A. 🎧 Listen and repeat.

1.
clap

2.
shout

3.
sing

4.
dance

B. 💿 Listen and point below. Then chant.

C. 💿 Listen and write the number.

Use the Action Words

A. 🎧 Listen and repeat.

Sing with me.

Sure.

B. 🎧 Listen and point below.

C. 🎧 Listen and point. Then sing along.

Word Time

9

A. 🎧 Listen and repeat.

1. swim
2. play soccer
3. ride a bike
4. jump rope
5. play baseball
6. climb a tree

B. 💿 Listen and point below. Then chant.

C. 💿 Listen and write the number.

Use the Words

A. 🎧 Listen and repeat.

I can climb a tree.

B. 🎧 Listen and point below.

C. 🎧 Listen and point. Then sing along.

Action Word Time

A. 🎧 Listen and repeat.

1.
throw the ball

2.
catch the ball

3.
hit the ball

4.
kick the ball

B. 🎧 Listen and point below. Then chant.

C. 🎧 Listen and write the number.

Use the Action Words

A. 🎧 Listen and repeat.

Watch me catch the ball.

B. 🎧 Listen and point below.

C. 🎧 Listen and point. Then sing along.

A. Listen and check.

1.
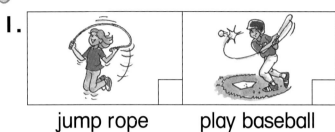
jump rope   play baseball

2.

play soccer   swim

3.

hungry   thirsty

4.
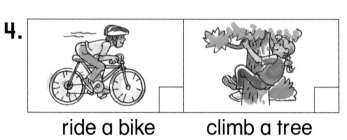
ride a bike   climb a tree

B. Listen and match.

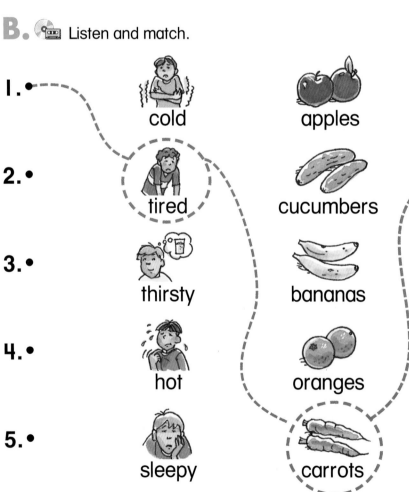

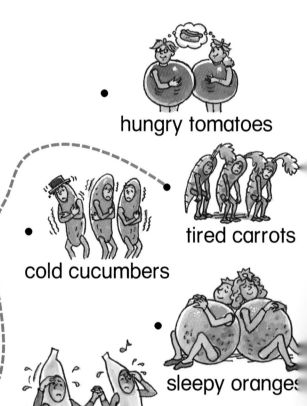

1. cold   apples   hungry tomatoes

2. tired   cucumbers   tired carrots

3. thirsty   bananas   cold cucumbers

4. hot   oranges   sleepy oranges

5. sleepy   carrots   hot bananas

6. hungry   tomatoes   thirsty apples

A. 🎧 Listen and match.

1.

   I'm hungry.

   I can dance.

2.

   I like oranges.

   Jump rope with me.

3.

   I can swim.

   I like green apples.

4.

   Let's eat together.

   I'm thirsty.

5.

   Sing with me.

   Watch me cook.

6.

   Watch me kick the ball.

   Let's play soccer together.

B. Role play these scenes with a partner.

Fall ABCs

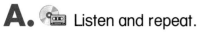

A. Listen and repeat.

N n — **n**est

O o — **o**ctopus

P p — **p**ig

Qq quilt   **Rr** rabbit   **Ss** sandwich

Word Time

A. Listen and repeat.

1.  rabbit
2.  dog
3.  turtle
4.  bird
5.  frog
6.  cat

B. Listen and point below. Then chant.

C. Listen and write the number.

Use the Words

A. 🔊 Listen and repeat.

I love my rabbit.

B. 🔊 Listen and point below.

C. 🔊 Listen and point. Then sing along.

Action Word Time

A. 🎧 Listen and repeat.

1.

fly

2.

jump

3.

hop

4.

run

B. 🎧 Listen and point below. Then chant.

C. 🎧 Listen and write the number.

Use the Action Words

A. 🎧 Listen and repeat.

B. 🎧 Listen and point below.

C. 🎧 Listen and point. Then sing along.

Word Time

A. Listen and repeat.

1. grandmother
2. mother
3. sister
4. grandfather
5. father
6. brother

B. Listen and point below. Then chant.

C. Listen and write the number.

Use the Words

A. 🎧 Listen and repeat.

This is my grandmother.

B. 🎧 Listen and point below.

C. 🎧 Listen and point. Then sing along.

Action Word Time

A. 🎧 Listen and repeat.

1.
wink

2.
whistle

3.
laugh

4.
cry

B. 💿 Listen and point below. Then chant.

C. 💿 Listen and write the number.

Use the Action Words

A. 🎧 Listen and repeat.

B. 🎧 Listen and point below.

C. 🎧 Listen and point. Then sing along.

Word Time

A. 🔊 Listen and repeat.

1.  clock

2. lamp

3. pillow

4. chair

5. bed

6. desk

B. 🔊 Listen and point below. Then chant.

C. 🔊 Listen and write the number.

Use the Words

A. 🎧 Listen and repeat.

This is a bed.

That is a chair.

B. 🎧 Listen and point below.

C. 🎧 Listen and point. Then sing along.

Action Word Time

A. 🔊 Listen and repeat.

1.
play

2.
read

3.
listen

4.
watch TV

B. 🔊 Listen and point below. Then chant.

C. 🔊 Listen and write the number.

Use the Action Words

A. 🎵 Listen and repeat.

Let's listen.

Good idea!

B. 💿 Listen and point below.

C. 💿 Listen and point. Then sing along.

A.  Listen and check.

1.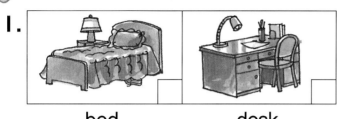

bed   desk

2.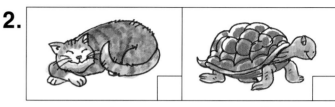

cat   turtle

3.

lamp   chair

4.

pillow   clock

B. 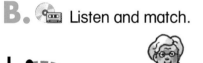 Listen and match.

1.

grandmother   dog   my mother and my dog

2.

father   rabbit   my brother and my cat

3.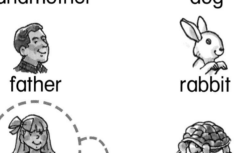

sister   turtle   my grandmother and my bird

4.

mother   cat   my father and my rabbit

5.

grandfather   frog   my grandfather and my turtle

6.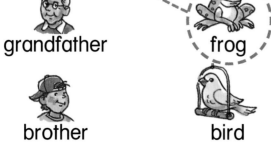

brother   bird   my sister and my frog

A. Listen and match.

1.

I love my dog.

Let's jump.

2.

This is my brother.

That is a frog.

3.

That is a chair.

Please don't run.

4.

It can fly.

This is my desk.

5.

Please don't laugh.

It can whistle.

6.

Let's play.

I love my mother.

B. Role play these scenes with a partner.

Winter ABCs

A. Listen and repeat.

Tt

turtle

Uu

umbrella

Vv

violin

Ww   **w**atch   Xx   bo**x**   Yy   **y**o-yo   Zz   **z**ebra

Songs and Chants

Numbers

The Counting Chant

One, One
Two, Two
Three, Three
Four, Four
Five, Five
Six, Six

One, Two, Three, Four, Five, Six

One, Two, Three * *
One, Two, Three * *
Four, Five, Six * *
Four, Five, Six * *

One, Two, Three * *
Four, Five, Six * *
One, Two, Three * *
Four, Five, Six * *

Unit 1

Word Time

The Name Chant

Digger * *
  Digger * *
Dot *
  Dot *
Annie * *
  Annie * *
Ted *
  Ted *

Digger, Dot, Annie, Ted
  Digger, Dot, Annie, Ted

(Repeat)

* * * * Yeah!
  * * * * Yeah!

Use the Words

The Hello Song

Hello! I'm Annie.
  Hello, hello, hello!

Hello! I'm Ted.
  Hello, hello, hello!

Hello, I'm Digger.
  Hello, hello, hello!

Hello, I'm Dot.
  Hello, hello, hello!

(Repeat)

Action Word Time

Shake Hands

Shake hands.
  Shake hands.

Smile, smile.
  Smile, smile.

Nod, nod.
  Nod, nod.

Wave, wave.
  Wave, wave.

Shake hands, smile, nod,
wave....Hello!

Use the Action Words

Let's Smile

(Melody: *Twinkle, Twinkle, Little Star*)

Let's smile.
Let's nod.
Let's wave.
Let's shake hands.

Let's smile.
Let's nod.
Let's wave.
Let's shake hands.

Unit 2

Word Time

The Shape Chant

Star, circle
  Star, circle

Circle, square
  Circle, square

Square, rectangle
  Square, rectangle

Rectangle, heart
  Rectangle, heart

Heart, triangle
  Heart, triangle

Triangle, star
  Triangle, star

Use the Words

I See a Star

(Melody: *Down by the Station*)

I see a star. I see a circle.
I see a heart. I see a square.
I see a triangle.
I see a rectangle.
* * * (*stomp, stomp*)
Hooray!

(Repeat)

Action Word Time

Walk, Walk

Walk.
  Walk.

Tiptoe.
  Tiptoe.

Dive.
  Dive.

Swim.
  Swim.

Walk, tiptoe, dive, swim!

Use the Action Words

Walk Over Here

Walk over here. * * *
Tiptoe over here. * * *
Dive over here. * * *
Swim over here. * * *

(Repeat)

Note: The symbol (*) that appears in some of the songs and chants represents handclaps.

Unit 3

Word Time

The Color Chant

Red * red * *
  Red * red * *

Black * black * *
  Black * black * *

Yellow * yellow * *
  Yellow * yellow * *

Green * green * *
  Green * green * *

Orange * orange * *
  Orange * orange * *

Blue * blue * *
  Blue * blue * *

Red *
  Red * *
Black *
  Black * *
Yellow *
  Yellow * *
Green *
  Green * *
Orange *
  Orange * *
Blue *
  Blue * *
* * * * * * Yeah!

Use the Words

It's Red

(Melody: *If You're Happy and You Know It*)

It's red. * *
  It's red. * *

It's blue. * *
  It's blue. * *

It's red.
  It's red.
It's blue.
  It's blue.

It's red. * * It's blue. * *

It's yellow. * *
  It's yellow. * *

It's green. * *
  It's green. * *

It's yellow.
  It's yellow.
It's green.
  It's green.

It's yellow. * * It's green. * *

It's orange. * *
  It's orange. * *

It's black. * *
  It's black. * *

It's orange.
  It's orange.
It's black.
  It's black.

It's orange. * * It's black. * *

Action Word Time

Paint, Paint, Paint

Paint, paint, paint.
  Paint, paint, paint.

Draw, draw, draw.
  Draw, draw, draw.

Color, color, color.
  Color, color, color.

Write, write, write.
  Write, write, write.

Paint.
  Paint.

Draw.
  Draw.

Color.
  Color.

Write.
  Write.

Use the Action Words

Write with Me

(Melody: *Mary Had a Little Lamb*)

Write with me.
Draw with me.
Color with me.
Paint with me.

Write with me.
Draw with me.
Color with me.
Paint with me.

(Repeat)

Spring ABCs

The Alphabet Chant A–F

A, /a/, apple
A, /a/, apple

B, /b/, bear
B, /b/, bear

C, /c/, cat
C, /c/, cat

D, /d/, dog
D, /d/, dog

E, /e/, elephant
E, /e/, elephant

F, /f/, fish
F, /f/, fish

A, B, C, D, E, F—oh yeah!

Unit 4

Word Time

Pencil, Eraser

Pencil, eraser * * *
  Pencil, eraser * * *

Book bag, book * * *
  Book bag, book * * *

Crayon, ruler * * *
  Crayon, ruler * * *

Pencil * eraser * book bag *
  Book * crayon * ruler *
Yeah!

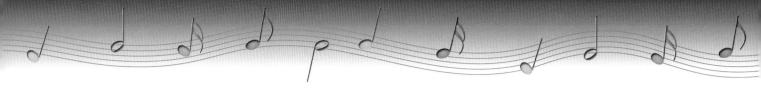

Use the Words

It's a Pencil

(Melody: *My Darling Clementine*)

It's a pencil.
It's a ruler.
It's a book bag.
It's a book!

It's an eraser.
It's a crayon.
It's a book bag.
It's a book!

It's a crayon.
It's a pencil.
It's a book bag.
It's a book!

It's a ruler.
It's an eraser.
It's a book bag.
It's a book!

Action Word Time

Open Your Book Bag

Open your book bag. * * *
   Open your book bag. * * *

Pick up your book. * * *
   Pick up your book. * * *

Put down your book. * * *
   Put down your book. * * *

Close your book bag. * * *
   Close your book bag. * * *

Open your book bag. * * *
Pick up your book. * * *
Put down your book. * * *
Close your book bag. Yeah!

Use the Action Words

The Book Bag Song

Open your book bag slowly.
Close your book bag quickly,
quickly.

Open your book bag quickly,
quickly.
Close your book bag slowly.

Pick up your book slowly.
Put down your book quickly,
quickly.

Pick up your book quickly,
quickly.
Put down your book slowly.

Unit 5

Word Time

The Numbers Chant

One, two
One, two

Three, four
Three, four

Five, six
Five, six

Seven, eight
Seven, eight

Nine, ten
Nine, ten

One, two, three
One, two, three

Four, five, six
Four, five, six

Seven, eight, nine
Seven, eight, nine

Ten!
Ten!

Hooray!

Use the Words

The Age Song

I'm two years old.
I'm four years old.
I'm six years old.
I'm eight years old.

I'm one year old.
I'm three years old.
I'm five years old.
I'm seven years old.

I'm nine years old.
I'm ten years old.
I'm four years old.

I'm three years old.
I'm two years old.
I'm one year old.

Action Word Time

Stand Up Chant

Stand up. * *
   Stand up. * *

Sit down. * *
   Sit down. * *

Kneel down. * *
   Kneel down. * *

Lie down. * *
   Lie down. * *

Stand up. * *
Sit down. * *
Kneel down. * *
Lie down. * *

(Repeat)

Use the Action Words

Stand Up, Sit Down

(Melody: *Mexican Hat Dance*)

Stand up, stand up, stand up.
   Okay.
Sit down, sit down, sit down.
   Okay.
Kneel down, kneel down,
kneel down.
   Okay.
Lie down, lie down, lie down.
   Okay.

Stand up, sit down, kneel down.
   Okay.
Lie down, stand up, sit down.
   Okay.
Kneel down, lie down, stand up.
   Okay.
Sit down, kneel down, lie down.
   Okay.

(Repeat first verse)

Unit 6

Word Time

Arms, Arms

Arms, arms. Legs, legs, legs.
Arms, arms. Legs, legs, legs.
Arms, arms. Legs, legs, legs.
Stop!

Hands, hands. Feet, feet, feet.
Hands, hands. Feet, feet, feet.
Hands, hands. Feet, feet, feet.
Stop!

Fingers, fingers. Toes, toes, toes.
Fingers, fingers. Toes, toes, toes.
Fingers, fingers. Toes, toes, toes.
Stop!

Use the Words

I Have Two Arms

I have two arms.
   Yeah, yeah!
I have two hands.
   Yeah, yeah!
I have ten fingers.
   Yeah, yeah!
It's me, it's me, it's me.

I have two legs.
   Yeah, yeah!
I have two feet.
   Yeah, yeah!
I have ten toes.
   Yeah, yeah!
It's me, it's me, it's me.

Action Word Time

Wash, Wash

Wash your hands.
   Wash, wash.
Dry your hands.
   Dry, dry.
Comb your hair.
   Comb, comb.
Brush your hair.
   Brush, brush.

Wash your hands.
   Hands, hands.
Dry your hands.
   Hands, hands.
Comb your hair.
   Hair, hair.
Brush your hair.
   Hair, hair.

Use the Action Words

Please Wash Your Hands

(Melody: *Out in the Woods
I Met a Bear*)

Please wash your hands.
   Please wash your hands.

Please dry your hands.
   Please dry your hands.

Please brush your hair.
   Please brush your hair.

Please comb your hair.
   Please comb your hair.

Please wash your hands.
Please dry your hands.
Please brush your hair.
Please comb your hair.

(Repeat)

Summer ABCs

The Alphabet Chant: G–M

G, /g/, goat
G, /g/, goat

H, /h/, horse
H, /h/, horse

I, /i/, iguana
I, /i/, iguana

J, /j/, juice
J, /j/, juice

K, /k/, kangaroo
K, /k/, kangaroo

L, /l/, lemon
L, /l/, lemon

M, /m/, monkey
M, /m/, monkey

G, H, I, J, K, L, M—oh yeah!

Unit 7

Word Time

Hot, Hungry

Hot, hungry. Hungry, hot.
   Hot, hungry. Hungry, hot.

Hot, thirsty. Thirsty, hot.
   Hot, thirsty. Thirsty, hot.

Hot, tired. Tired, hot.
   Hot, tired. Tired, hot.

Hot, sleepy. Sleepy, hot.
   Hot, sleepy. Sleepy, hot.

Cold, hungry. Hungry, cold.
   Cold, hungry. Hungry, cold.

Cold, thirsty. Thirsty, cold.
   Cold, thirsty. Thirsty, cold.

Cold, tired. Tired, cold.
   Cold, tired. Tired, cold.

Cold, sleepy. Sleepy, cold.
   Cold, sleepy. Sleepy, cold.

Use the Words

I'm Hungry

I'm hungry. I'm hungry.
   I'm hot. * *

I'm thirsty. I'm thirsty.
   I'm hot. * *

I'm tired. I'm tired.
   I'm hot. * *

I'm sleepy. I'm sleepy.
   I'm hot. * *

I'm hungry. I'm hungry.
   I'm cold. * *

I'm thirsty. I'm thirsty.
   I'm cold. * *

I'm tired. I'm tired.
   I'm cold. * *

I'm sleepy. I'm sleepy.
   I'm cold. * *

Action Word Time

Eat, Drink

Eat, drink. * *
Cook, clean up. * *
Eat, * drink, * cook, * clean up. * *

Eat, drink. * *
Cook, clean up. * *
Eat, * drink, * cook, * clean up. * *

Eat, drink. * *
Cook, clean up. * *
Eat, * drink, * cook, * clean up. * *

Use the Action Words

Let's Cook Together

Let's cook together,
together, together.
Let's cook together.
Hooray, hooray, hooray!

Let's eat together,
together, together.
Let's eat together.
Hooray, hooray, hooray!

Let's drink together,
together, together.
Let's drink together.
Hooray, hooray, hooray!

Let's clean up together,
together, together.
Let's clean up together.
Hooray, hooray, hooray!

Unit 8

Word Time

Apples, Oranges

Apples, oranges
Oranges, apples
Apples, oranges
Yum! Yum!

Carrots, cucumbers
Cucumbers, carrots
Carrots, cucumbers
Yum! Yum!

Tomatoes, bananas
Bananas, tomatoes
Tomatoes, bananas
Yum! Yum!

Apples, oranges
Carrots, cucumbers
Tomatoes, bananas
Yum! Yum!

Use the Words

I Like Apples

(Melody: *Ode to Joy*)

I like apples.
I like oranges.
I like carrots.
Yum! Yum! Yum!

I like apples.
I like oranges.
I like carrots.
Yum! Yum! Yum!

I like bananas.
I like tomatoes.
I like cucumbers.
Yum! Yum! Yum!

I like apples.
I like oranges.
I like carrots.
Yum! Yum! Yum!

I like bananas.
I like tomatoes.
I like cucumbers.
Yum! Yum! Yum!

I like apples.
I like oranges.
I like carrots.
Yum! Yum! Yum!

Action Word Time

Dance, Sing

Dance, sing.
  Dance, sing.
Shout! Shout!
Clap, clap, clap!

Dance, sing.
  Dance, sing.
Shout! Shout!
Clap, clap, clap!

Sing, dance.
  Sing, dance.
Clap! Clap!
Shout, shout, shout!

Sing, dance.
  Sing, dance.
Clap! Clap!
Shout, shout, shout!

Use the Action Words

Sing with Me

Sing with me.
  Sure.
Dance with me.
  Sure.
Shout with me.
  Sure.
Clap with me.
  Sure.

  La! La! La!
Sing with me.
  (*tap, tap, tap*)
Dance with me.
  Hip! Hip! Hooray!
Shout with me.
  (*clap, clap, clap*)
Clap with me.

(*Repeat first verse*)

Unit 9

Word Time

The Action Chant

Play soccer, play baseball,
play soccer. * *
Ride a bike. * *
Ride a bike. * *

Play baseball, play soccer,
play baseball. * *
Climb a tree. * *
Climb a tree. * *

Play soccer, play baseball,
play soccer. * *
Jump rope. * *
Jump rope. * *

Play baseball, play soccer,
play baseball. * *
Swim, swim, swim. * *

Use the Words

I Can Swim

(Melody: *The Farmer in the Dell*)

I can swim.
I can swim.
Swim, swim, swim, swim.
I can swim.

I can jump rope.
I can jump rope.
Jump, jump, jump, jump.
I can jump rope.

I can play soccer.
I can play soccer.
Play, play, play, play.
I can play soccer.

I can play baseball.
I can play baseball.
Play, play, play, play.
I can play baseball.

I can ride a bike.
I can ride a bike.
Ride, ride, ride, ride.
I can ride a bike.

I can climb a tree.
I can climb a tree.
Climb, climb, climb, climb.
I can climb a tree.

Action Word Time

The Ball Chant

The ball * *
The ball * *
Throw the ball.
Throw the ball.
Throw, throw, throw…

The ball * *
The ball * *
Hit the ball.
Hit the ball.
Hit, hit, hit…

The ball * *
The ball * *
Catch the ball.
Catch the ball.
Catch, catch, catch…

The ball * *
The ball * *
Kick the ball.
Kick the ball.
Kick, kick, kick…

…the ball!

Use the Action Words

Watch Me

(Melody: *The Hokey-Pokey*)

Watch me throw the ball.
Watch me catch the ball.
Watch me hit the ball.
Watch me kick the ball.
    Throw, throw, throw,
    throw.
Watch me throw the ball.

Watch me throw the ball.
Watch me catch the ball.
Watch me hit the ball.
Watch me kick the ball.
    Catch, catch, catch,
    catch.
Watch me catch the ball.

Watch me throw the ball.
Watch me catch the ball.
Watch me hit the ball.
Watch me kick the ball.
    Hit, hit, hit, hit.
Watch me hit the ball.

Watch me throw the ball.
Watch me catch the ball.
Watch me hit the ball.
Watch me kick the ball.
    Kick, kick, kick, kick.
Watch me kick the ball.

Fall ABCs

The Alphabet Chant: N–S

N, /n/, nest
N, /n/, nest

O, /o/, octopus
O, /o/, octopus

P, /p/, pig
P, /p/, pig

Q, /q/, quilt
Q, /q/, quilt

R, /r/, rabbit
R, /r/, rabbit

S, /s/, sandwich
S, /s/, sandwich

N, O, P, Q, R, S—oh yeah!

Unit 10

Word Time

Animal Chant

A frog, a dog
A frog, a dog

A dog, a frog
A dog, a frog

A cat, a bird
A cat, a bird

A bird, a cat
A bird, a cat

A rabbit, a turtle
A rabbit, a turtle

A turtle, a rabbit
A turtle, a rabbit

Use the Words

I Love My Rabbit

(Melody: *Sing a Song of Sixpence*)

I love my rabbit.
I love my frog.
I love my turtle.
I love my dog.
I love my bird.
I love my cat.

Rabbit, turtle, dog.
Bird, frog, cat.

(Repeat)

Action Word Time

Run, Run, Run

Jump! Jump!
  Run, run, run!
Jump! Jump!
  Run, run, run!
Jump! Jump!
  Run, run, run!
Jump! Jump! Stop!

Hop! Hop!
  Run, run, run!
Hop! Hop!
  Run, run, run!
Hop! Hop!
  Run, run, run!
Hop! Hop! Stop!

Fly! Fly!
  Run, run, run!
Fly! Fly!
  Run, run, run!
Fly! Fly!
  Run, run, run!
Fly! Fly! Stop!

Use the Action Words

It Can Run!

(Melody: *Do You Know the Muffin Man?*)

It can run.
  Run, run, run.
It can run.
  Run, run, run.
It can run.
  Run, run, run.
It can run!

It can jump.
  Jump, jump, jump.
It can jump.
  Jump, jump, jump.
It can jump.
  Jump, jump, jump.
It can jump!

It can hop.
  Hop, hop, hop.
It can hop.
  Hop, hop, hop.

It can hop.
  Hop, hop, hop.
It can hop!

It can fly.
  Fly, fly, fly.
It can fly.
  Fly, fly, fly.
It can fly.
  Fly, fly, fly.
It can fly!

Unit 11

Word Time

Father, Father

Father, father * * *
Mother, mother * * *
Father, * mother *
Father, * mother *

Sister, sister * * *
Brother, brother * * *
Sister, * brother *
Sister, * brother *

Grandmother * * *
Grandfather * * *
Grandmother, * grandfather *
* * * Hooray!

Use the Words

The Family Song

(Melody: *I'm a Little Teapot*)

This is my mother.
Yes, oh yes!
This is my sister.
Yes, oh yes!
This is my grandmother.
Yes, oh yes!
* * * * Yes, oh yes!

This is my father.
Yes, oh yes!
This is my brother.
Yes, oh yes!
This is my grandfather.
Yes, oh yes!
* * * * Yes, oh yes!

Action Word Time

Laugh, Laugh, Laugh

Laugh, laugh, laugh.
(Ha-ha!)
  Cry, cry, cry.
  (Boo-hoo!)
Laugh, laugh, laugh.
(Ha-ha!)
  Cry, cry, cry.
  (Boo-hoo!)

Whistle, whistle, whistle.
(*whistling sound*)
  Wink, wink, wink.
  (*winking sound*)
Whistle, whistle, whistle.
(*whistling sound*)
  Wink, wink, wink.
  (*winking sound*)

Laugh, laugh, laugh.
(Ha-ha!)
Cry, cry, cry.
(Boo-hoo!)
Whistle, whistle, whistle.
(*whistling sound*)
Wink, wink, wink.
(*winking sound*)

Use the Action Words

Please Don't Laugh

Please don't laugh.
  Sorry.
Please don't laugh.
  Sorry.
Please don't laugh.
  Sorry.
Please don't laugh.

Please don't whistle.
  Sorry.
Please don't whistle.
  Sorry.
Please don't whistle.
  Sorry.
Please don't whistle.

Please don't cry.
  Sorry.
Please don't cry.
  Sorry.
Please don't cry.
  Sorry.
Please don't cry.

Please don't wink.
   Sorry.
Please don't wink.
   Sorry.
Please don't wink.
   Sorry.
Please don't wink.

Unit 12

Word Time

Lamp, Clock

Lamp, clock
Lamp, clock
   Clock, clock...
Tick tock!

Clock, lamp
Clock, lamp
   Clock, clock...
Tick tock!

Desk, chair
Desk, chair
   Clock, clock...
Tick tock!

Chair, desk
Chair, desk
   Clock, clock...
Tick tock!

Pillow, bed
Pillow, bed
   Clock, clock...
Tick tock!

Bed, pillow
Bed, pillow
   Clock, clock...
Tick tock!

Use the Words

This, That!

(Melody: *Humpty Dumpty*)

Lamp, lamp, this is a lamp.
Chair, chair, that is a chair.
Lamp, lamp.
   Chair, chair.
This is a lamp.
   That is a chair.

Clock, clock, that is a clock.
   Bed, bed, this is a bed.
Clock, clock.
   Bed, bed.
That is a clock.
   This is a bed.

Pillow, pillow, this is a pillow.
Desk, desk, that is a desk.
Pillow, pillow.
   Desk, desk.
This is a pillow.
   That is a desk.

Action Word Time

Watch TV

Watch TV, watch TV.
   Play, play. * * *

Watch TV, watch TV.
   Read, read. * * *

Watch TV, watch TV.
   Listen, listen. * * *

Watch TV, watch TV.
Play, play.
Read, read.
Listen, listen

* And watch TV! * *

Use the Action Words

Good Idea!

(Melody: *If You're Happy and You Know It*)

Let's play. * *
   Good idea! * *
Let's play. * *
   Good idea! * *
Let's play. Let's play.
   Good idea! Good idea!
Let's play. * *
   Good idea! * *

Let's read. * *
   Good idea! * *
Let's read. * *
   Good idea! * *
Let's read. Let's read.
   Good idea! Good idea!
Let's read. * *
   Good idea! * *

Let's listen. * *
   Good idea! * *
Let's listen. * *
   Good idea! * *
Let's listen. Let's listen.
   Good idea! Good idea!
Let's listen. * *
   Good idea! * *

Let's watch TV.
   Good idea! * *
Let's watch TV.
   Good idea! * *
Let's watch TV.
   Good idea! Good idea!
Let's watch TV.
   Good idea! * *

Winter ABCs

The Alphabet Chant T–Z

T, /t/, turtle
T, /t/, turtle

U, /u/, umbrella
U, /u/, umbrella

V, /v/, violin
V, /v/, violin

W, /w/, watch
W, /w/, watch

X, /x/, box
X, /x/, box

Y, /y/, yo-yo
Y, /y/, yo-yo

Z, /z/, zebra
Z, /z/, zebra

T, U, V, W, X, Y, Z—oh yeah!

Word List

A

a	9
and	64
Annie	4
apple	18
apples	40
arms	28

B

ball	46
bananas	40
baseball	44
bear	18
bed	60
bike	44
bird	52
black	12
blue	12
book	20
book bag	20
box	67
brother	56
brush	30

C

can	45
carrots	40
cat	18, 52
catch	46
chair	60
circle	8
clap	42
clean up	38
climb	44
clock	60
close	22
cold	36
color	14
comb	30
cook	38
crayon	20
cry	58
cucumbers	40

D

dance	42
desk	60
Digger	4
dive	10
dog	19, 52
don't	59
Dot	4
draw	14
drink	38
dry	30

E

eat	38
eight	24
elephant	19
eraser	20

F

fall	50
father	56
feet	28
fingers	28
fish	19
five	24
fly	54
four	24
frog	52

G

goat	34
good idea	63
grandfather	56
grandmother	56
green	12

H

hair	30
hands	28
have	29
heart	8
hello	5
here	11
hit	46
hop	54
horse	34
hot	36
hungry	36

I

I	9
iguana	34
I'm	5
is	57

J

juice	35
jump	54
jump rope	44

K

kangaroo	35
kick	46
kneel down	26

L

lamp	60
laugh	58
legs	28
lemon	35
let's	7
lie down	26
like	41
listen	62
love	53

M

me	15
monkey	35
mother	56
my	53

N

nest	50
nine	24
nod	6

O

octopus	50
okay	27
one	24
open	22
orange	12
oranges	40
over	11

P

paint	14
pencil	20
pick up	22
pig	50
pillow	60
play	44, 62
please	31
put down	22

Q

quickly	23
quilt	51

R

rabbit	51, 52
read	62
rectangle	8
red	12
ride	44
ruler	20
run	54

S

sandwich	51
see	9
seven	24
shake hands	6
shout	42
sing	42
sister	56
sit down	26
six	24
sleepy	36
slowly	23
smile	6
soccer	44
sorry	59
spring	18
square	8
stand up	26
star	8
summer	34
sure	43
swim	10

T

Ted	4
ten	24
that	61
the	46
thirsty	36
this	57
three	24

U

throw	46
tiptoe	10
tired	36
toes	28
together	39
tomatoes	40
tree	44
triangle	8
turtle	52, 66
TV	62
two	24

U

umbrella	66

V

violin	66

W

walk	10
wash	30
watch	67
watch me	47
watch TV	62
wave	6
whistle	58
wink	58
winter	66
with	15
write	14

Y

years old	25
yellow	12
your	22
yo-yo	67

Z

zebra	67